weblinks

You don't need a computer to use this book. But, for readers who do have access to the Internet, the book provides links to recommended websites which offer additional information and resources on the subject.

You will find weblinks boxes like this on some pages of the book.

weblinks

For more information about eyes and sight, go to www.waylinks.co.uk/series/ourbodies/senses

waylinks.co.uk

To help you find the recommended websites easily and quickly, weblinks are provided on our own website, **waylinks.co.uk.** These take you straight to the relevant websites and save you typing in the Internet address yourself.

Internet safety

Website content

HODDER
Wayland

OUR BODIES

THE SENSES

Steve Parker

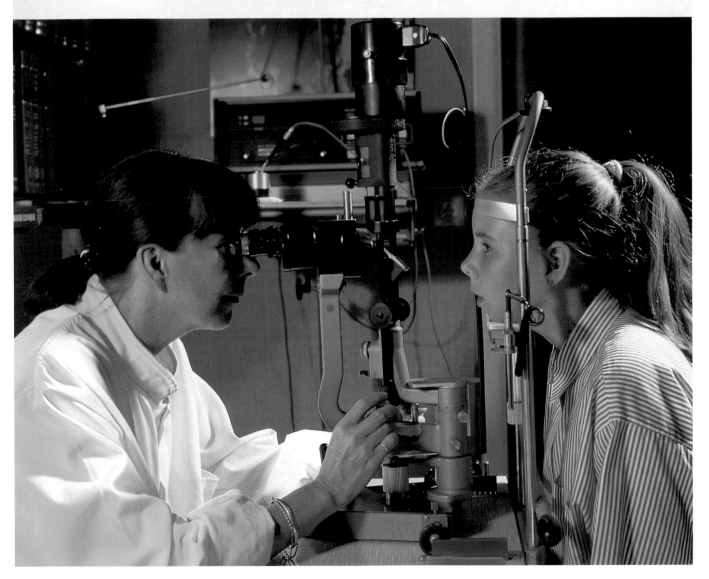

HODDER
Wayland

an imprint of Hodder Children's Books

Titles in the series:
The Brain and Nervous System • Digestion
The Heart, Lungs and Blood • Reproduction
The Senses • The Skeleton and Muscles

Produced by Monkey Puzzle Media Ltd
Gissing's Farm, Fressingfield, Suffolk IP21 5SH, UK

Text copyright © 2003 Steve Parker
Series copyright © 2003 Hodder Wayland
First published in 2003 by Hodder Wayland
an imprint of Hodder Children's Books

Commissioning Editor: Victoria Brooker
Book Editor: Nicola Edwards
Design: Jane Hawkins
Picture Research: Sally Cole
Artwork: Alex Pang
Consultant: Dr Trish Groves

British Library Cataloguing in Publication Data
Parker, Steve, 1952–
  The Senses. – (Our bodies)
  1. Senses and sensation – Juvenile literature
  I.Title
  612.8

  ISBN 07502 3675 2

Printed and bound in Hong Kong

Hodder Children's Books
A division of Hodder Headline Limited
338 Euston Road, London NW1 3BH

Picture Acknowledgements
Action Plus 38 (Neil Tingle); Alamy 5 (ImageState), 18 (Jim Pickerell/Stock Connection Inc), 22 (Wilmar Photography.com), 41 (Novastock/Stock Connection Inc); Corbis front cover main image (Charles Gupton), 4 (Bojan Brecelj), 7 (Stephen Frink), 44 Bob Krist; Corbis Digital Stock 23 top (Marty Snyderman); Digital Vision 9 top; FLPA 15 top (Tony Hamblin), 31 Minden Pictures; Rex Features 24 (Reso), 42 (Clive Dixon); Robert Harding Picture Library 19 bottom (Adam Woolfitt), 45 (Vaughan Bean); Science Photo Library front cover inset (Omikron), 1 (CC Studio), 9 bottom (Omikron), 10 (Andrew McClenaghan), 13 top (James King-Holmes), 13 bottom (Ralph Eagle), 16 (CC Studio), 17 (Stanford Eye Clinic), 21 bottom, 25 (James King-Holmes), 26, 29 (BSIP Vem), 37 (J C Revy), 39 (Astrid and Hanns-Frieder Michler).

CONTENTS

INTRODUCTION

Senses at work

Every day we look at scenes and screens, and listen to sounds like music and people speaking. We smell scents and odours, eat tasty meals, and embrace a loved one or stroke a pet. But we rarely pause to wonder how we carry out all these activities, and how the body's senses work to receive information about the world around us.

A stimulating event – the body's senses respond to the loud music, bright lights, sweaty odours and jostling crowds at the music club.

If one sense is faulty or lacking, another may be able to compensate, as in the touch-reading system called Braille for those with poor or no vision.

FIVE MAIN SENSES

The body's five main senses are sight (vision), hearing, smell, taste and touch. Each of these major senses has body parts called sense organs or sensors. They are specialized to detect a feature or change outside the body. For example in sight, the eyes detect light rays, and for hearing, the ears pick up sound waves. The nose is sensitive to tiny odour particles floating in air, while the tongue detects flavour particles in food.

SIGNALS TO THE BRAIN

As the sense organs detect these features outside the body, they produce patterns of tiny electrical pulses, called nerve signals, inside the body. These signals are sent along nerves to the brain, which sorts and processes them. It is not in the sense organ, but in the brain, that we become aware of what our senses detect, and where we realize what is happening around us.

MORE SENSES

The body's senses are much more complicated than they seem. For example, the skin is the sense organ of touch or feeling. But it detects far more than physical contact with objects, when it is touched or pressed. It can also feel heat, cold, movements and pain. Also, balance is sometimes called a sense. But it is really a process that goes on all the time, using information from various sense organs such as the skin, eyes, inner ears, and also tiny stretch sensors in muscles and joints.

EYES AND SIGHT

Most important

For most people, sight or vision is the most important sense. Closing your eyes makes it hard to move about safely or carry out everyday tasks like writing, and it's impossible to read or watch TV. More than half the knowledge and information in the brain, stored as memories, probably came in through the eyes as pictures, words, scenes and other sights.

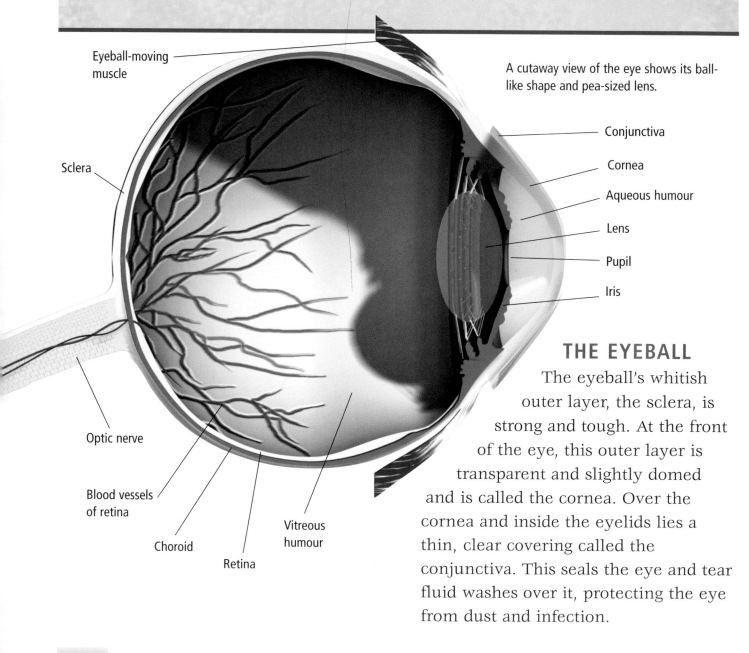

A cutaway view of the eye shows its ball-like shape and pea-sized lens.

Eyeball-moving muscle

Sclera

Optic nerve

Blood vessels of retina

Choroid

Retina

Vitreous humour

Conjunctiva

Cornea

Aqueous humour

Lens

Pupil

Iris

THE EYEBALL

The eyeball's whitish outer layer, the sclera, is strong and tough. At the front of the eye, this outer layer is transparent and slightly domed and is called the cornea. Over the cornea and inside the eyelids lies a thin, clear covering called the conjunctiva. This seals the eye and tear fluid washes over it, protecting the eye from dust and infection.

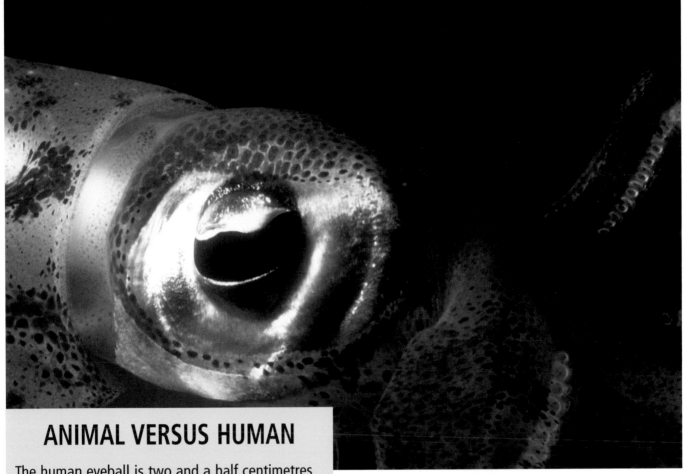

ANIMAL VERSUS HUMAN

The human eyeball is two and a half centimetres across. The biggest animal eye belongs to the giant squid. It's over 20 centimetres across – almost the size of a football!

Squid have huge eyes for their body size, to see well in the dark depths of the ocean. They chase after prey such as small fish, using sight as their main hunting sense.

PUPIL AND LENS

The iris is a coloured ring mainly of muscle behind the cornea. The dark-looking hole in the middle is the pupil. The iris adjusts the size of the pupil, according to light conditions. Usually the pupil gets larger in dim light, to allow more light into the eye and give a brighter view. Just behind the pupil is the lens. Like the lens in a camera, it focuses the light rays to form a clear, sharp picture inside the eyeball (see next page).

Try this!

Study your own eyes in a mirror – the sclera (white), iris (coloured part) and pupil (dark hole). Close your eyes for 15 seconds, then open them and carefully watch the pupil. With the eye closed, the pupil opens wider, to try and let in more light. As soon as the eye opens, the iris makes the pupil shrink, to stop too much light from entering.

Light rays to nerve signals

Light rays shine into the eye through the clear cornea at the front, then through the hole called the pupil, and the clear, curved lens behind it. Between the cornea and lens is a narrow space filled with fluid called aqueous humour, which is continually being made and absorbed. Then the light passes into the middle of the eyeball. This is filled with a clear, jelly-like fluid, vitreous humour. It gives the eyeball its rounded shape and slightly squishy feel.

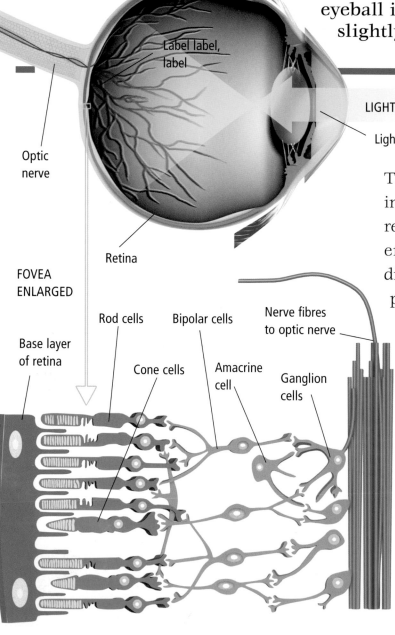

Label label, label

Optic nerve

LIGHT RAYS

Light rays pass through pupil and lens

Retina

FOVEA ENLARGED

Base layer of retina

Rod cells

Cone cells

Bipolar cells

Amacrine cell

Nerve fibres to optic nerve

Ganglion cells

The rays then shine onto the curved inner lining of the eyeball, known as the retina. This is the part that changes the energy from light rays, with their different colours and brightness, into patterns of nerve signals which are sent to the brain. Between the retina and the eye's tough outer covering, the sclera, is a middle layer called the choroid. This has many blood vessels that help to nourish the retina and sclera.

LIGHT RAYS

A series of cell layers in the retina process nerve signals from the rods and cones.

INSIDE THE RETINA

The retina is bowl-shaped, about twice the area of a fingernail, and as thick as this page of paper. Yet it contains many millions of microscopic parts called rod cells and cone cells. These make nerve signals when light rays shine onto them. The 125 million rod cells are spread evenly through most of the retina. The seven million cone cells are mainly packed closely into a tiny area known as the fovea or yellow spot, in the middle of the retina at the back of the eye. When the eye looks directly at an object, the image of the object shines onto the fovea. This is the area of the retina where vision is clearest and sharpest, because the numerous closely-packed cones can detect colours and tiny details (see next page).

— **weblinks** —

To find out more about eyes and sight, go to
www.waylinks.co.uk/series/ourbodies/senses

MICRO-BODY

In the retina, the cone cells are slightly shorter and have pointed ends, while the rod cells are longer with blunter ends. Most of the cones are packed into a tiny area called the fovea, which is in the middle of the retina, facing the lens and pupil.

Cone cells (greenish) nestle among the taller rod cells (blue).

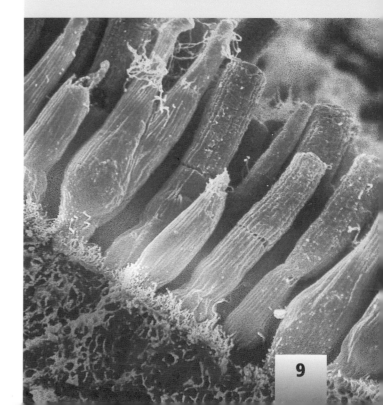

MOVEMENTS AND COLOURS

FAST-CHANGING IMAGES

Cinema films are sometimes called 'movies', meaning 'moving pictures'. But the pictures are not really moving. They are still images, like photographs. These are flashed onto the screen very quickly, one after the other, 25 or 30 every second. Each picture, or frame, is slightly different from the one before. But the light-sensitive rod and cone cells in the eye's retina cannot work fast enough to detect the pictures as single still images. As a result, the fast-changing images merge or blur together, to give the impression of continuous movement.

THREE COLOURS FOR CONES

The rod cells in the retina do not distinguish any colours. They detect all colours equally. But they do distinguish different light levels, from bright to dull, and so they see in black and white. The cone cells are specialized to detect colours. There are three types of cone cells – red, green and blue. These are not the colours of the cones themselves, but the colours of light they detect. Pure red light makes only the 'red' cones work. Pure green light

Problems with colour vision can be detected using special charts made of dots with different hues. The most common form of colour vision defect is being unable to distinguish between certain shades of red and green in dim light (see page 17).

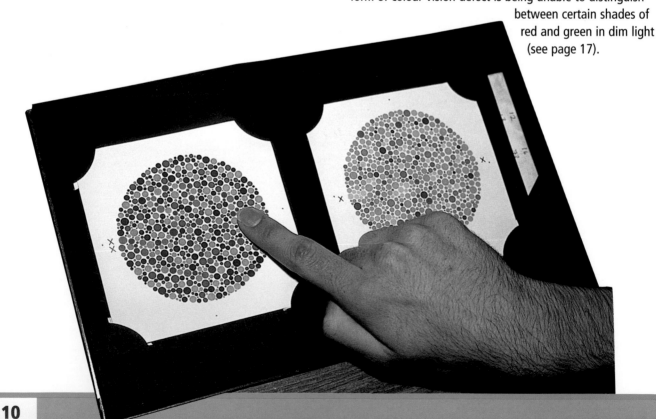

affects only 'green' cones. Pure blue light causes 'blue' cones to make nerve signals. Other colours of light are made up of mixtures of red, green and blue light, so they make combinations of cone cells work. For example, yellow light is a mixture of red and green light, so it makes red and green cones work at the same time. The brain works out the colours and shades of light from the varying combinations of signals sent to it by the different types of cones.

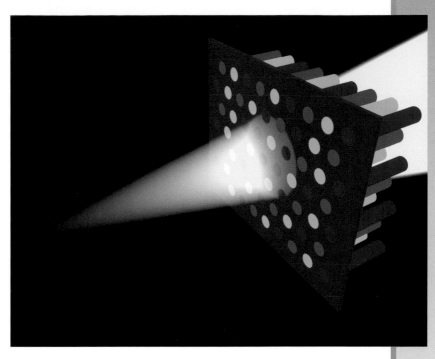

White light is a mixture of all colours, so it makes all three kinds of cone cells in the retina respond – red, green and blue.

Try this!

In a small notebook or notepad, draw a simple image like a stick-person, in the middle or lower corner of each page. Move the arms and legs slightly from one page to the next, as if the person is walking. Flick the pages slowly and the eye can detect each picture separately. Flick them faster and see how the stick-person seems to move more smoothly, as the eye merges the images together. This is what happens when we watch TV and cinema screens.

Make the flicker-drawing simple and easy to copy from one page to the next.

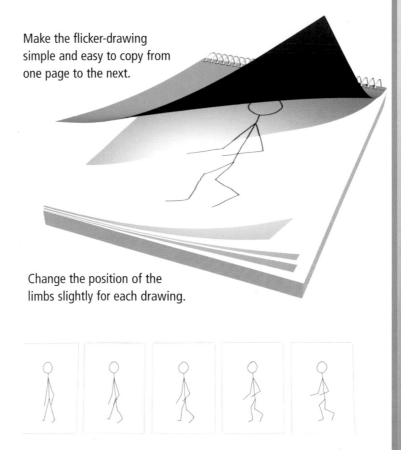

Change the position of the limbs slightly for each drawing.

Judging distance

We use our eyes to see colours, shapes, patterns and movements, and also to judge distances. When we look at an object, both eyes point straight towards it. If the object is quite near, the eyes must point slightly inwards. The nearer the object, the greater the inward angle of each eye, which is called the angle of convergence (see below).

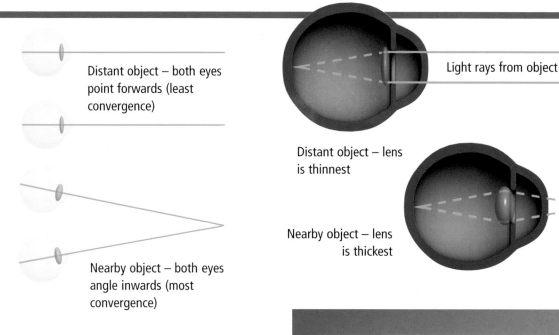

Distant object – both eyes point forwards (least convergence)

Nearby object – both eyes angle inwards (most convergence)

Light rays from object

Distant object – lens is thinnest

Nearby object – lens is thickest

The angle at which the eyes point inwards is known as convergence, while the lens' changing shape for focusing is termed accommodation. Both help us to assess distance.

The eyeball is moved by six tiny muscles behind it. These muscles have sensors in them to detect how short or long they are. As the eyes swivel to look inwards at a nearby object, the muscles on the outside of the eye are stretched longer, and the brain detects this. It can then work out the eye's angle of convergence to judge the distance of the object.

Try this!

See how the eyes swivel and change their angle of convergence to judge distance, with the help of a friend. The friend holds a pen at arm's length and looks straight at it, then gradually moves the pen closer. See how the friend's eyes gradually look inwards more and more. When the pen is very close, the angle of convergence is greatest – and the friend looks very 'cross-eyed'!

TWO EYES

The two eyes look at an object from different positions, so they have slightly different views of it. You can see this if you look at a nearby object with one eye only, then with the other eye. Notice how the two views are slightly different. The nearer the object, the more different the two views of it. The brain compares the two images and this also helps to judge its distance.

Frequent eye tests are part of the many health checks undergone by pilots, who must be able to see clearly both distant objects, like the runway, and nearer ones such as the dials and controls.

MICRO-BODY

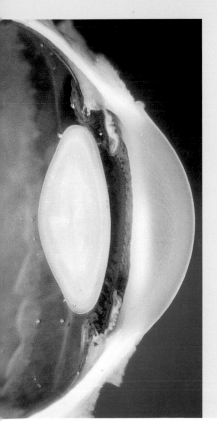

A camera's lens moves its position to focus the image clearly. The eye's lens does not move, but it does become fatter or thinner. The lens is suspended by tiny thread-like ligaments within a ring of muscle, the ciliary muscle, which alters its shape.

Tiny, shadowy, pale threads of ciliary ligaments link the yellow-coloured lens to the pale brown bulges of ciliary muscle.

LOOKING THROUGH THE LENS

A camera's lens is adjusted to give a clear, sharp view of a nearby object or a faraway one. This is called focusing. The eye also adjusts its lens to focus on near or far objects – this is known as accommodation. The eye's lens focuses by changing its shape. A ring-shaped ciliary muscle around the lens contracts to make the ring smaller, and the lens more bulging, to focus on nearby objects. To focus on faraway objects, the ciliary muscle relaxes into a larger ring, and stretches the lens thinner. Like the eye-moving muscles, the ciliary muscles have stretch sensors in them. Signals from these sensors pass to the brain, which can work out the shape of the lens, and so judge the distance of the object.

THE MIND'S EYE

A complicated network

The eye's millions of rods and cones produce billions of nerve signals every second. But these do not go straight to the brain. The rods and cones are connected to a layer of nerve cells in the retina known as bipolar cells, which are, in turn, linked to another layer, the ganglion cells. In addition, yet more cells link groups of rods and cones, and groups of ganglion cells. All of these cells are within the retina. The result is an amazingly complicated network which works like a computer to process and combine nerve signals (see also page 8).

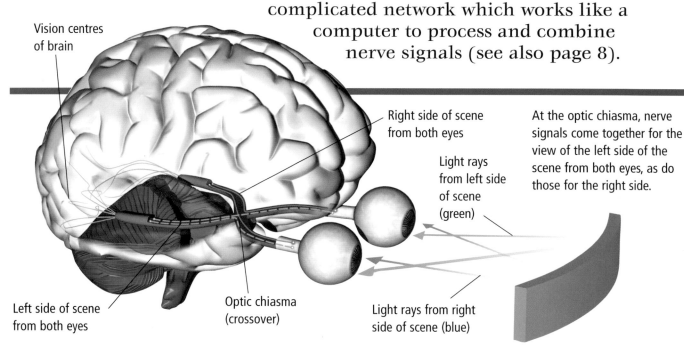

Vision centres of brain

Right side of scene from both eyes

Light rays from left side of scene (green)

At the optic chiasma, nerve signals come together for the view of the left side of the scene from both eyes, as do those for the right side.

Left side of scene from both eyes

Optic chiasma (crossover)

Light rays from right side of scene (blue)

FROM EYE TO BRAIN

The nerve signals from all over the retina travel along one million nerve fibres. These come together in one small area to form the start of the optic nerve. This area of the retina has no rods or cones, so cannot detect light. It is known as the 'blind spot'. In daily life, the eyes dart about rapidly, so the missing patch of the scene from the blind spot is continually 'filled in' and we do not notice it.

Try this!

With one eye closed, look straight at the cross with the other eye, holding the page 30 centimetres away. Gradually bring it closer. Keep looking at the cross, but also notice the dot – it disappears when its image falls on your eye's blind spot.

●

INSIDE THE BRAIN

The optic nerves join to the lower front of the brain, at the optic chiasma or 'crossover'. Here, nerve signals from one eye are 'shared' with signals from the other eye. This makes it easier for the brain to compare the views in both eyes. The signals then pass to the lower rear brain surface, known as the visual cortex or vision centres. This area works out what the signals mean as shapes, colours, lines, angles, curves and shades, and puts them together as the final scene.

ANIMAL VERSUS HUMAN

Animal eyes work in various ways. The frog's eye has rod cells grouped into patches called 'bug detectors'. These are specialized to detect small, fast-moving objects like flies.

Frogs see small objects if they move fast, but not if they stay still – so a stationary fly is safe until it moves.

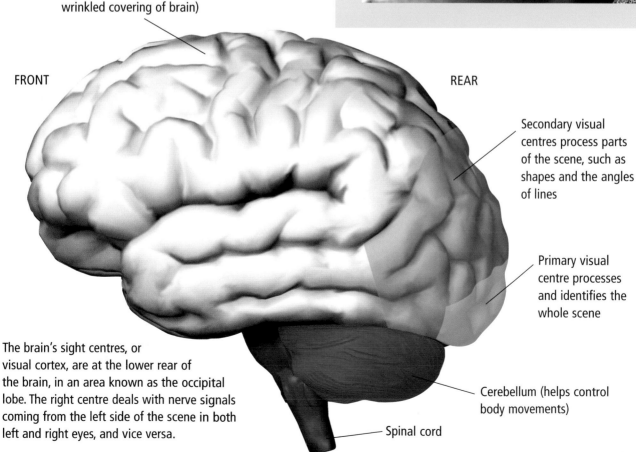

Cerebral cortex (main wrinkled covering of brain)

FRONT

REAR

Secondary visual centres process parts of the scene, such as shapes and the angles of lines

Primary visual centre processes and identifies the whole scene

The brain's sight centres, or visual cortex, are at the lower rear of the brain, in an area known as the occipital lobe. The right centre deals with nerve signals coming from the left side of the scene in both left and right eyes, and vice versa.

Cerebellum (helps control body movements)

Spinal cord

VISION PROBLEMS

A precious sense

Eyes are very delicate, and sight is a most precious sense. Loss of sight, for a person who could previously see well, can have enormous and restricting effects on everyday life. It's advised to have a regular eye examination, usually by an expert called an ophthalmic optician, who can shine a light through the pupil to see the retina within.

The ophthalmic optician uses various machines to check the eye's health, including the pressure inside the eyeball.

Top Tips

The eyes are at risk from fast-moving objects such as a ball in sport, windblown sand or grit, or tiny sharp pieces or shards, for example, when using a metal-grinding machine. The risk of injury can be greatly reduced by wearing eye protection such as a mask.

SIGHT DISORDERS

Some vision problems occur because the lens is the wrong shape in relation to the whole eyeball. In short sight (myopia), the eyeball is too large for the lens, so the person cannot see faraway objects clearly. In long sight (hypermetropia), the eyeball is too small in relation to the lens, so nearby objects look blurred. An extra contact or spectacle lens helps the eye's own lens to focus more clearly. Around eight in 100 males and one in 200 females are 'colour blind'. Usually this means they cannot distinguish between two colours, most often red and green, because of an inherited fault with their cone cells. It is very rare to see no colours at all, and only shades of grey.

GLAUCOMA, CATARACT AND DIABETES

In glaucoma, too much fluid (aqueous humour) collects in front of the eyeball. This increases the pressure in the eyeball and can damage the retina. In a cataract, the lens becomes opaque and looks white or 'misty'. Both disorders are more common in older people and can usually be treated successfully, especially with high-precision laser surgery. Diabetes is a condition in which the body is unable to use its main energy source, blood sugar, properly. It can damage small blood vessels in various parts of the body,

MICRO-BODY

An eye expert shines a light through the pupil to illuminate the inside of the eyeball, and looks through the eye's own lens which magnifies the view of the interior.

This optician's 'eye view' shows the tiny blood vessels which branch across the retina.

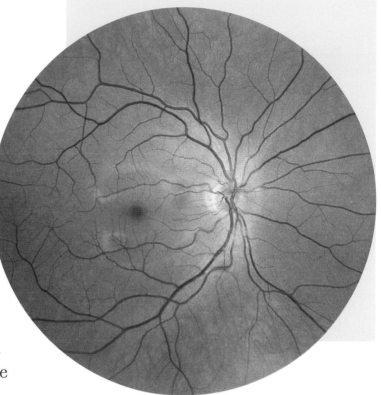

including the retina. Regular eye checks and careful control of diabetes can lessen the risk of this eye problem, known as diabetic retinopathy.

weblinks

To find out more about vision problems, go to www.waylinks.co.uk/series/ourbodies/senses

EARS AND HEARING

An automatic filter

Sound travels as waves through the air, water and objects. It is detected by the organs of hearing or auditory sense – our ears. But we do not notice or remember every sound we hear. The brain automatically filters out common and familiar sounds which are less important, like the background noise of traffic or the wind. This allows the mind to concentrate on sounds that might be more important.

Look, listen and learn – hearing is a vital part of the way children gain new information and understanding, especially at school and when chatting with friends.

Try this!

Cup your hands over your ears, fingers together. Sounds are much quieter and more muffled, because your hands block the sound waves. Rub your ears with your hands, and hear how loud these sounds are. The rubbing causes vibrations, which pass directly through the skin and skull bone to the inner ear, without the need for sound waves.

OUTER EAR

The ear is much more than the part you can see on the side of the head. This is the pinna, a flap of skin-covered cartilage (gristle). It funnels sound waves into the ear canal, a tube leading

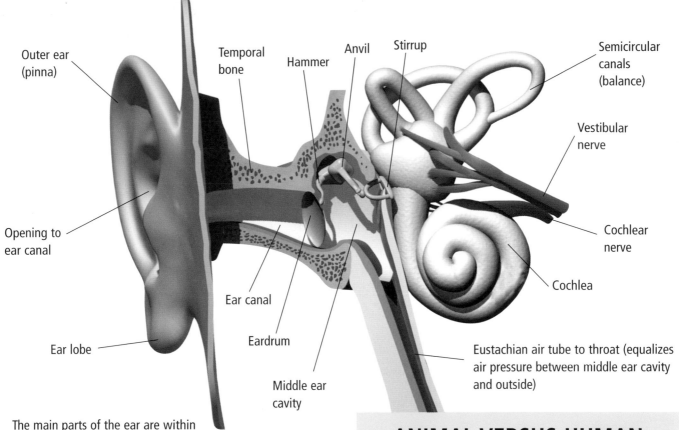

Outer ear (pinna)

Temporal bone

Hammer

Anvil

Stirrup

Semicircular canals (balance)

Vestibular nerve

Opening to ear canal

Cochlear nerve

Cochlea

Ear lobe

Ear canal

Eardrum

Middle ear cavity

Eustachian air tube to throat (equalizes air pressure between middle ear cavity and outside)

The main parts of the ear are within the thickness of the part of the skull called the temporal bone.

about two centimetres into the skull bone. The canal ends at the eardrum, a taut flap of thin skin the size of the little fingernail. Sound waves bounce off the eardrum and make it shake.

MIDDLE EAR

On the inner side of the eardrum is the middle ear cavity, containing three tiny bones called the hammer, anvil and stirrup. These are the auditory ossicles – the smallest bones in the body. They are joined end-to-end, with the hammer touching the eardrum and the stirrup touching part of the inner ear called the cochlea. Vibrations pass from the eardrum along the ossicles to the cochlea, where nerve signals are made.

ANIMAL VERSUS HUMAN

Human ears have limits. Some sounds are too quiet, too high or too deep for us to hear. Certain animals, like dogs and horses, have better hearing than us and easily detect sounds which we cannot.

A dog pricks up its ears at a faint, faraway sound, but its human owner can hear nothing.

Changing patterns

Deep in the ear, patterns of sound vibrations are changed into patterns of nerve signals in the curled, snail-shaped part called the cochlea. This is well protected by skull bone almost all around it. The stirrup bone vibrates against a thin, flexible part of the cochlea, the oval window. When the oval window vibrates, this sends ripples into the fluid inside the cochlea.

Semicircular canals (balance)

Vestibular nerves (balance)

A small section cut out of the cochlea (left) is enlarged (below) to show the three passageways or ducts running through it, and the spiral organ of Corti, which is then enlarged further (opposite).

Cochlear nerve (hearing)

Basal whorl of cochlea

Duct system within cochlea

Apex (upper tip) of cochlea

Utricle (balance)

Saccule (balance)

ENLARGED VIEW OF COCHLEA

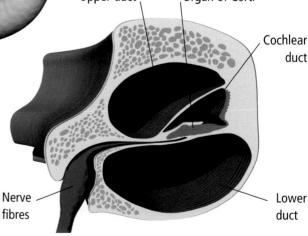

Upper duct

Organ of Corti

Cochlear duct

Nerve fibres

Lower duct

Top Tips

The ear canal's lining makes wax, to which dust and dirt stick. As the jaw joints near the ears move, when speaking and chewing, the flakes of wax naturally work their way out of the canal. Very occasionally, too much wax or a tiny object gets stuck in the canal. A doctor or other medical worker should remove this. Never try to poke it out yourself, even with a cotton wool bud. You may damage the eardrum.

MICRO-HAIRS

Inside the cochlea, curled around like a corkscrew, is the spiral organ of Corti. This has two main layers or membranes, one on top of the other. The bottom one, the basilar membrane, has about 25,000 tiny cells called hair cells, in

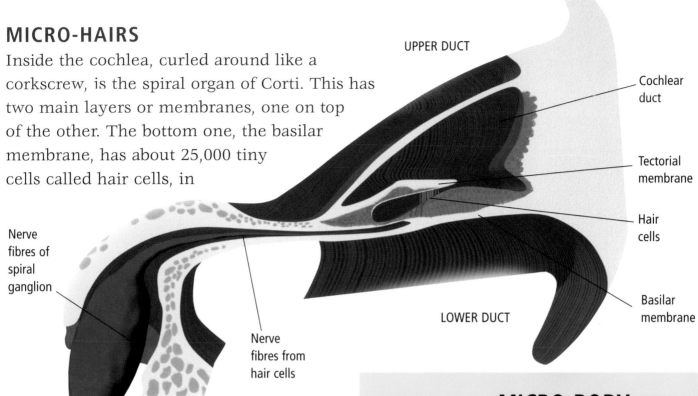

Cochlear duct

Tectorial membrane

Hair cells

Basilar membrane

LOWER DUCT

Nerve fibres of spiral ganglion

Nerve fibres from hair cells

Inside the cochlea, the spiral organ of Corti has two membranes with thousands of hair cells between.

four rows along its length. Sticking up from each cell are 50 or more short micro-hairs. The hair tips stick into the upper layer, the tectorial membrane.

SOUNDS TO SIGNALS

Ripples from the sound vibrations pass through the fluid inside the cochlea. They cause the membranes to flex or bend up and down, and the micro-hairs to shake. As the micro-hairs move, the hair cells they project from make nerve signals. These pass along the hair cell nerve fibres, which gather together to become the cochlear nerve. The nerve carries the signals to the hearing centre or auditory cortex on the side of the brain.

MICRO-BODY

The hair cells in the organ of Corti are arranged in four rows. Three are outer hair cells and the micro-hairs of each one form a U-shaped pattern. The inner hair cells have their micro-hairs arranged in a line.

The micro-hairs of the hair cells stick into the tectorial membrane.

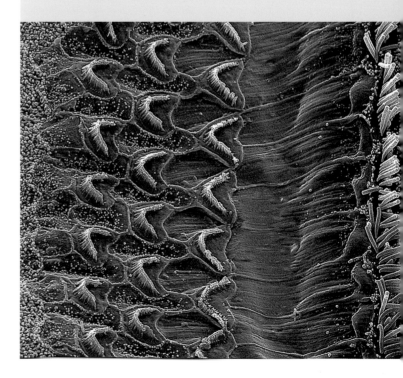

21

WHERE'S THAT NOISE?

In the rainforest, sight is very limited – but sounds can warn of approaching danger.

SOUND IDENTIFICATION

Imagine you are walking through a forest on a very dark night. You need to rely more on your ears than your eyes. Your mind concentrates on every tiny sound, working out its various features, trying to identify it and what it means. One feature is loudness or volume. Deep in the ear, in the cochlea, sound vibrations make the membranes and micro-hairs move. Louder sounds make bigger vibrations. So the membranes and micro-hairs move further, making more nerve signals.

Try this!

Many sounds reach the ear after bouncing, or reflecting, off surfaces like walls and floors. In a room with hard walls and a hard floor (not carpet), ask a friend to clap hands in different places – near the wall, high up and low down. Stand in the middle, eyes closed. Hear how the claps differ in volume and how the sounds bounce or echo. Can you point to the correct direction of the clap each time?

HIGH AND LOW

Another feature is pitch – the high or low quality of sound. Higher-pitched sounds make faster vibrations. Some parts of the cochlear membranes bend more with high-pitched sounds, while other parts are affected by low-pitched sounds. Like volume, pitch changes the patterns of nerve signals being sent to the brain.

DIRECTION OF SOUND

Sounds travel through air at about 330 metres per second. This means a sound coming from one side reaches the nearer ear a split second before it gets to the farther ear. Also, because it passes straight into the ear canal of the nearer ear, it is louder there, compared to the other ear canal facing the other direction. The brain detects these tiny differences in timing and loudness, and works out a sound's direction.

ANIMAL VERSUS HUMAN

Whales and dolphins use clicks, squeals and groans to communicate messages. Water carries sound waves much faster and farther than air, and some whale songs travel more than 100 kilometres through the ocean. Imagine shouting that far on land!

A humpback whale sings its eerie moaning love-song.

weblinks

To find out more about ears and hearing, go to
www.waylinks.co.uk/series/ourbodies/senses

Louder sounds (bigger waves) reach nearer ear first

Quieter sounds (smaller waves) reach farther ear later

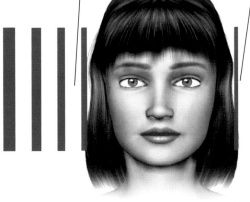

Loudness or volume of sound fades with distance

A sound which comes from one side is louder and earlier in the ear on that side compared to the other ear. The brain can detect the time difference, which is less than one-thousandth of a second.

HEARING PROBLEMS

Tests and treatment

Some people may not be aware that they have difficulty in hearing. Signs of hearing loss include the need to turn up the television or music system louder than other people, and asking speakers to repeat what they have said when other people around have heard clearly. Simple tests by a doctor or other medical staff can check if there is a problem. Then a specialist, known as an audiologist, can do further tests and suggest treatment, such as a hearing aid or, in some cases, an operation.

EAR INFECTIONS

Sometimes germs (harmful microbes) multiply in the outer, middle or inner ear. The germs that cause a sore throat can spread along a channel called the Eustachian tube from the back of the

Ear-defenders are part of the vital protective equipment for many noisy jobs, such as grinding metal and sawing wood.

Top Tips

Too-loud sounds, especially if high-pitched and long-lasting, can damage the internal ear's delicate structures, sometimes permanently. There are usually regulations to limit loud sounds in places like nightclubs and factories. People who work with noisy machines wear ear-defenders to protect their hearing.

throat to the middle ear. There they cause otitis media, infecting the middle ear and making it swollen and filled with pus. This may press on and burst the eardrum. Germs which cause a common cold or sinusitis (affecting air spaces in the bones of the face) can also spread to the ear.

GLUE EAR

Long-term ear infection can leave sticky fluid in the middle ear. This 'glue ear' may not cause much pain. But it can affect hearing, by hampering vibration of the ear bones. This can cause special problems during childhood, when children are learning to speak and to listen. Sometimes a child thought to have learning difficulties actually has glue ear or another hearing problem. Most ear infections clear up on their own, perhaps with the need for painkillers to treat the symptom of earache. But severe infection may need antibiotic treatment or even surgery.

HEARING DIFFICULTY

In otosclerosis, bony growths restrict the movements of the stirrup, so it cannot pass its vibrations to the cochlea. In this and certain other ear disorders, a hearing aid may help. Or the stirrup may be freed by an

operation, or even replaced with an artificial version. In the rare event of severe cochlear damage, a cochlear implant can partly restore hearing, as long as there are still some intact nerve fibres. The implant is a tiny electronic device inserted into the inner ear and connected by wires to a receiver under the scalp. It detects vibrations, and mainly helps the person to hear their own voice.

MICRO-BODY

In one form of cochlear implant a behind-the-ear microphone sends signals to a transmitter on the scalp, which passes them to a receiver within the head.

The implant is under the wheel-like transmitter.

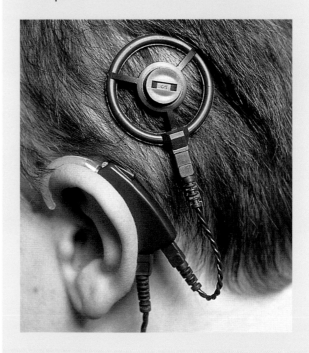

SMELL AND TASTE

Sniff the air

We usually notice the sense of smell (olfaction) less than other senses – until we sniff a strong odour such as a powerful perfume – or well-rotted manure! The nose detects common and everyday smells, but the brain often filters them out, so the mind can concentrate on new or changing odours which might be important.

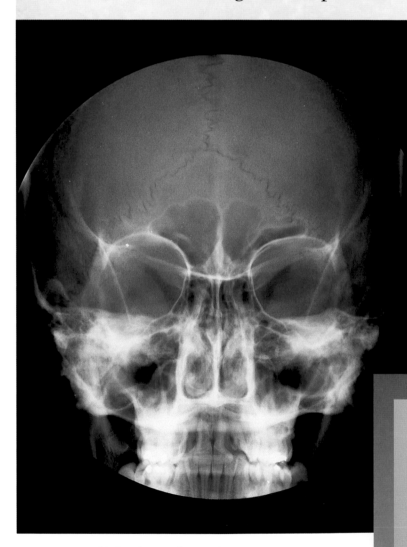

In this head X-ray the nasal chambers show up as the dark regions between the lower parts of the eyes.

For example, when you enter a place with a strong smell, like a flower shop, your nose detects it. But then the smell seems to fade, and may seem to disappear after a few minutes. The smell is still there, and just as strong, but you have 'got used' to it. This is known as habituation. It happens with sounds, touches and tastes too.

Try this!

When you breathe normally, air passes through the lower parts of the nasal chambers. Few odorant particles reach the olfactory areas in the upper part, so smells are weaker. If you sniff, air swirls higher into the roof of the nasal chamber, nearer the olfactory areas, so the smell is stronger. Try breathing normally near something smelly like a flower, perfume or air-freshener, then sniff more deeply and see how the odour becomes stronger.

FLOATING IN AIR

Tiny odorant particles, too small to see, float about in the air. Every breath takes air into the nasal chambers, which are two thumb-sized air spaces in the skull, one behind each side of the nose. The parts that detect the odorant particles are in the lining of the top or roof of the nasal chamber. They are called the olfactory areas or olfactory epithelia (see next page).

(see next page)

ANIMAL VERSUS HUMAN

Some animals rely more on their noses, than on their eyes. The mole lives in darkness and its eyes are tiny, almost useless. But its nose is long and quivering, and always sniffing for food or danger.

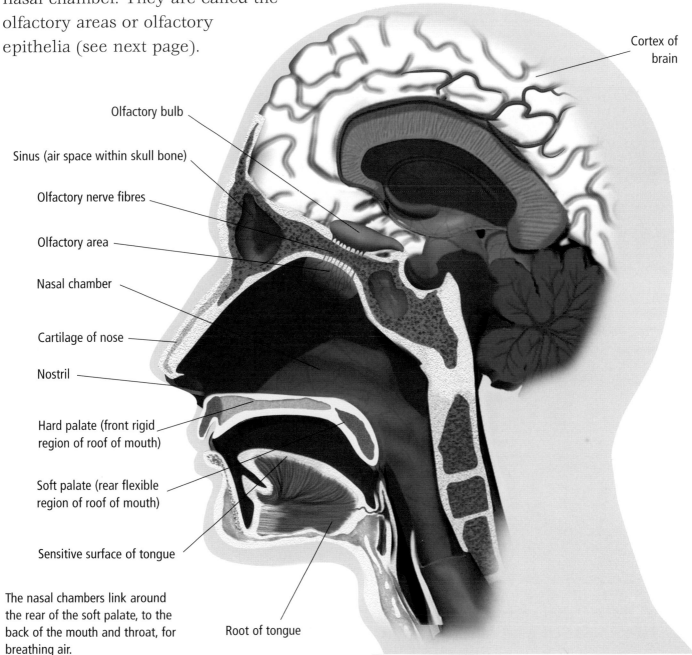

Cortex of brain

Olfactory bulb

Sinus (air space within skull bone)

Olfactory nerve fibres

Olfactory area

Nasal chamber

Cartilage of nose

Nostril

Hard palate (front rigid region of roof of mouth)

Soft palate (rear flexible region of roof of mouth)

Sensitive surface of tongue

The nasal chambers link around the rear of the soft palate, to the back of the mouth and throat, for breathing air.

Root of tongue

SCENTS SENSE AND GOOD TASTE

Olfactory cells

Each olfactory area is about the size of a thumbnail, containing some 20 million microscopic cells called olfactory cells. Each cell has 10–20 micro-hairs, named cilia, sticking out from its surface. The cilia project into the thin layer of mucus (slimy fluid) which coats the whole inner lining of the nasal chamber.

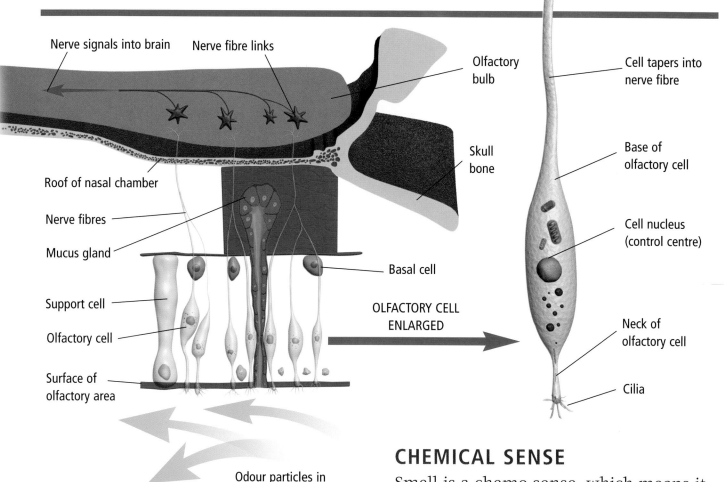

Nerve signals into brain

Nerve fibre links

Olfactory bulb

Cell tapers into nerve fibre

Roof of nasal chamber

Skull bone

Nerve fibres

Base of olfactory cell

Mucus gland

Basal cell

Cell nucleus (control centre)

Support cell

OLFACTORY CELL ENLARGED

Olfactory cell

Neck of olfactory cell

Surface of olfactory area

Cilia

Odour particles in nasal chamber

The olfactory area contains thousands of olfactory cells, support cells and other cells. The microscopic hair-like cilia of each olfactory cell stick from its surface into the mucus and air stream within the nasal chamber below.

CHEMICAL SENSE

Smell is a chemo-sense, which means it is a body sense that detects chemicals – the tiny floating particles called odorants. Each type of smell is probably carried by a different type of odorant chemical with its own shape. These

28

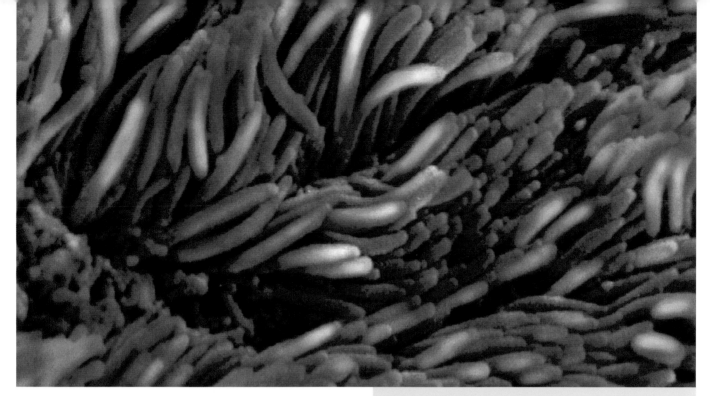

The mucus coating the smell-detecting cilia has been removed in this micro-photograph.

particles fit into receptors or 'landing sites' which cover the cilia that stick down from the olfactory cells. If a particular odorant chemical fits into a same-shaped receptor, like a key into a lock, this causes the olfactory cell to make nerve signals.

TO THE BRAIN

Like other sense organs, the olfactory areas send signals along nerve fibres. These pass through the thin layer of skull bone just above, to a large, bulging collection of nerves known as the olfactory bulb, under the front of the brain. Here the signals are partly sorted and combined, before travelling along the olfactory nerve, into the brain itself.

MICRO-BODY

The microscopic cilia that project from the 20-plus million olfactory cells form a thick 'carpet' that is coated with slimy mucus. Odorant particles must seep or dissolve into the mucus, before they can fit into 'landing sites' or receptors on the cilia, and thereby generate nerve signals.

Try this!

Our memory for smells is powerful – perhaps because the memory and smell centres in the brain are near each other and have plentiful connections. For example, sniff a pine-scented air freshener – and you may imagine pine forests.

weblinks
To find out more about smell and taste, go to www.waylinks.co.uk/series/ourbodies/senses

TIP OF THE TONGUE

Safety checks

Taste (gustation) is, like smell, a chemo-sense. The tongue detects tiny particles of chemicals called flavorants, in foods and drinks. So like smell, taste allows us to check foods before we eat them. If a food smells and tastes odd or unusual, we tend to avoid it. Long ago, when foods were gathered from the wild, this was a useful way of checking whether berries, fruits and other items were safe to eat. Today, smell and taste are used more for pleasure, as we enjoy our meals, snacks and drinks.

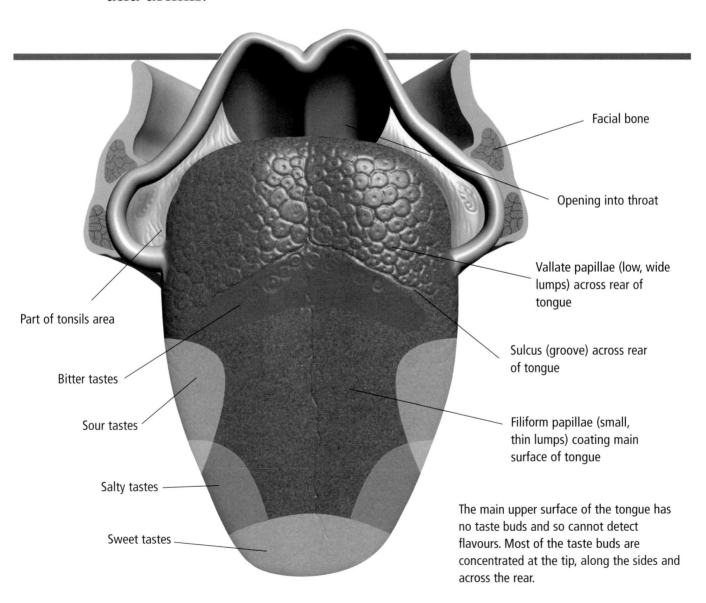

Facial bone

Opening into throat

Vallate papillae (low, wide lumps) across rear of tongue

Sulcus (groove) across rear of tongue

Filiform papillae (small, thin lumps) coating main surface of tongue

Part of tonsils area

Bitter tastes

Sour tastes

Salty tastes

Sweet tastes

The main upper surface of the tongue has no taste buds and so cannot detect flavours. Most of the taste buds are concentrated at the tip, along the sides and across the rear.

FEWER FLAVOURS THAN ODOURS

Tastes are detected by microscopic taste buds (see next page) spread along the sides and back of the tongue. They work in a similar way to the olfactory cells in the nose. However, they tell apart only four basic flavours – sweet, salty, sour and bitter. All other flavours are combinations of these four, in varying amounts. In contrast, the nose can tell apart many thousands of different smells and odours.

Try this!

You need a drinking straw, some sugar, and clean water to rinse your mouth between each test. Use the straw to put a few grains of sugar on the tip of your tongue, but do not move it. Can you detect the sweet flavour? After rinsing, put some grains on the side of the tongue. Is the sweetness as strong? Try the back of the tongue. Can you detect any sweetness at all? The diagram opposite shows which part of the tongue is sensitive to sugar.

ANIMAL VERSUS HUMAN

An anteater not only tastes with its tongue, it catches food too. Its tongue is very long (up to 60 centimetres) and very sticky. It flicks out several times each second, to lick up hundreds of ants and termites every minute.

An anteater can hardly open or close its small jaws. It eats with its tongue, licking up small insects which stick to the plentiful slimy mucus coating the tongue.

Gripping and tasting

The tongue has small lumps and pimples called papillae over much of its surface. These papillae help the tongue to grip slippery food as this is mixed with saliva (spit) and chewed. But the parts of the tongue that do the tasting are much smaller than the papillae. They are microscopic taste buds, and they number about 10,000. Most of the taste buds are around the sides and bases of the papillae, along the edges of the tongue and across its rear. There are also a few taste buds on the insides of the cheeks and lips. The main central area of the tongue has no taste buds and so cannot detect any flavours.

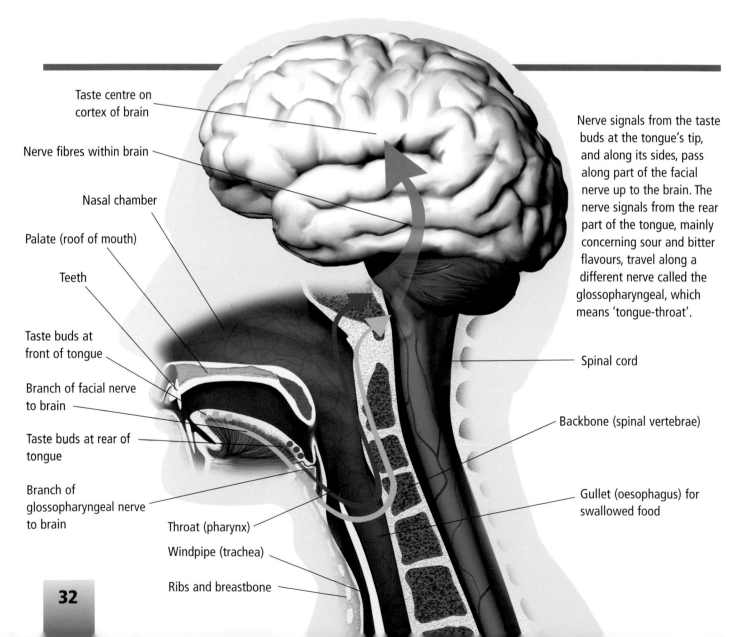

Taste centre on cortex of brain

Nerve fibres within brain

Nasal chamber

Palate (roof of mouth)

Teeth

Taste buds at front of tongue

Branch of facial nerve to brain

Taste buds at rear of tongue

Branch of glossopharyngeal nerve to brain

Throat (pharynx)

Windpipe (trachea)

Ribs and breastbone

Nerve signals from the taste buds at the tongue's tip, and along its sides, pass along part of the facial nerve up to the brain. The nerve signals from the rear part of the tongue, mainly concerning sour and bitter flavours, travel along a different nerve called the glossopharyngeal, which means 'tongue-throat'.

Spinal cord

Backbone (spinal vertebrae)

Gullet (oesophagus) for swallowed food

ANOTHER CHEMO-SENSE

Each taste bud is like a tiny orange, with about 50 cells as the segments. Half of these are gustatory or taste-sensing cells, and each one has several micro-hairs, cilia, sticking from its tip. Particular shapes of flavorant particles in food fit into the same-shaped receptors or 'landing sites' on the cilia, like keys into their locks, and this makes the gustatory cell produce nerve signals. The signals pass along nerve fibres to the taste areas on each side of the brain, called the gustatory cortex.

Flavour particles dissolved in saliva seep through tiny holes in the tongue's surface, called taste pores, to reach the taste buds below. The hair-like cilia at the upper end of each gustatory cell detect the particles.

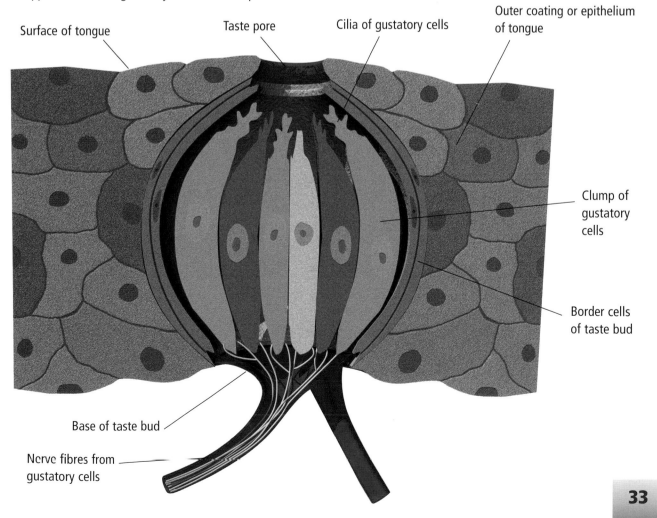

Surface of tongue

Taste pore

Cilia of gustatory cells

Outer coating or epithelium of tongue

Clump of gustatory cells

Border cells of taste bud

Base of taste bud

Nerve fibres from gustatory cells

SMELL AND TASTE PROBLEMS

Strongly linked

Smell and taste are separate senses, and their nerve signals travel to different parts of the brain. But both these senses are usually important at the same time, when we eat and drink. Also, odours from chewed food float up from the back of the mouth, around the rear of the palate, and into the nasal chamber, where they are smelled. For this reason, odours and flavours become strongly linked in the mind. What we imagine as the 'taste' of a food is a combination of taste and smell. When a common cold blocks the nose, it cannot detect food odours. Then it seems like food tastes of very little. In fact it tastes normal, but the added interest of its smells is missing.

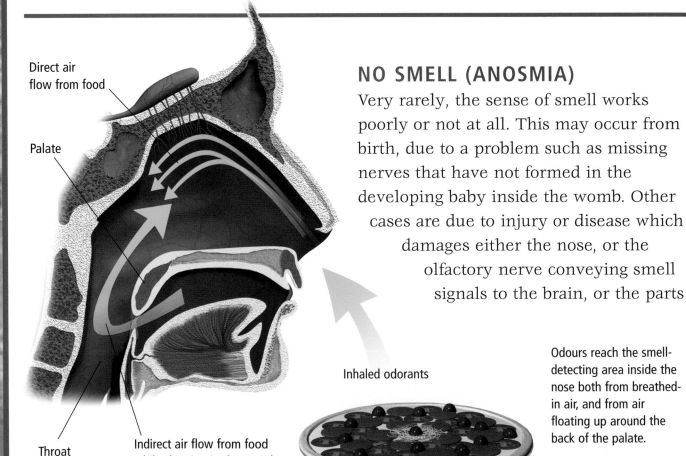

Direct air flow from food

Palate

Throat

Indirect air flow from food while chewing in the mouth

Inhaled odorants

NO SMELL (ANOSMIA)

Very rarely, the sense of smell works poorly or not at all. This may occur from birth, due to a problem such as missing nerves that have not formed in the developing baby inside the womb. Other cases are due to injury or disease which damages either the nose, or the olfactory nerve conveying smell signals to the brain, or the parts

Odours reach the smell-detecting area inside the nose both from breathed-in air, and from air floating up around the back of the palate.

of the brain where smell signals are analyzed. The same can happen with taste.

SENSING NOTHING

Some medicines and other drugs, and also some mental (mind-based) conditions, can affect the way the brain deals with smells, tastes or other senses. The sense may seem blunted and duller, or keener and 'heightened'. Or the mind is tricked into experiencing odours, flavours, sights, sounds or touches that do not exist. These are called sensory hallucinations.

Try this!

Taste a strong flavour like a powerful peppermint. Then straight away, taste a more delicate flavour, like a banana. See how the stronger taste (and smell) alters the more delicate one. Some people swish out their mouths with water or an ice-sorbet, between the courses of a meal, so that tastes do not linger and affect later flavours.

Taste centre (gustatory cortex) on outside of brain

Cortex (wrinkled surface of brain)

Smell centre (olfactory cortex) inside brain

The main areas for analyzing taste nerve signals are on the sides of the brain, in the surface layer or cortex. The smell centres are also in the cortex, but where it folds underneath and then up, on the inside of the brain.

weblinks

To find out more about smell and taste problems, go to www.waylinks.co.uk/series/ourbodies/senses

THE SENSE OF TOUCH

Strange feelings

Touch one of your hands with the fingertips of the other. The hand feels warm, dry and slightly soft. Dip the hand in cold water and try again. Now it feels cooler, wet and slippery. The sense of touch provides far more information than whether part of the body is in contact with something. It distinguishes hard from soft, rough from smooth, warm from cold, wet from dry, sticky from slippery, and still from moving.

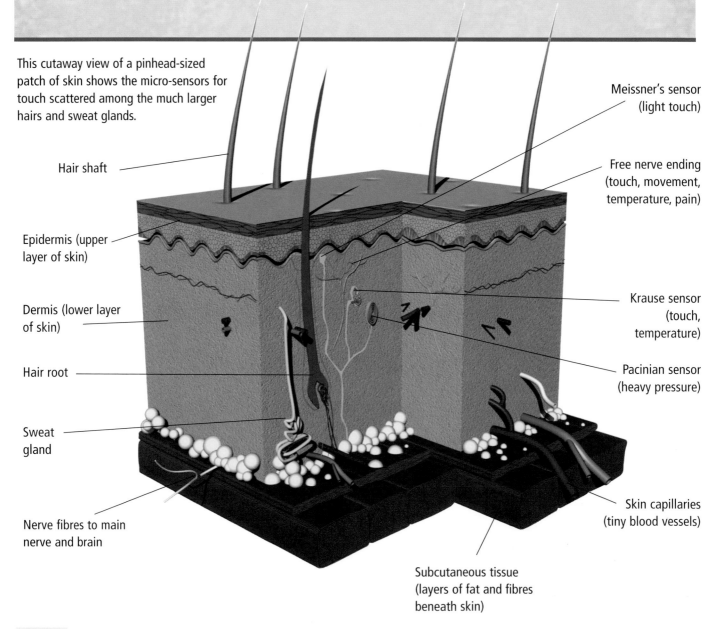

This cutaway view of a pinhead-sized patch of skin shows the micro-sensors for touch scattered among the much larger hairs and sweat glands.

Hair shaft

Epidermis (upper layer of skin)

Dermis (lower layer of skin)

Hair root

Sweat gland

Nerve fibres to main nerve and brain

Meissner's sensor (light touch)

Free nerve ending (touch, movement, temperature, pain)

Krause sensor (touch, temperature)

Pacinian sensor (heavy pressure)

Skin capillaries (tiny blood vessels)

Subcutaneous tissue (layers of fat and fibres beneath skin)

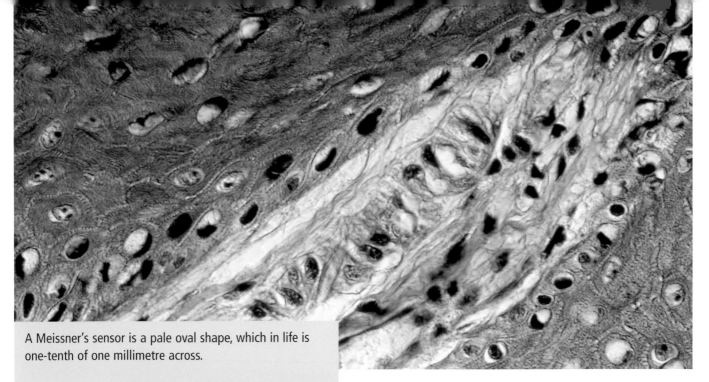

A Meissner's sensor is a pale oval shape, which in life is one-tenth of one millimetre across.

MICRO-BODY

The different micro-sensors in skin are placed at different levels, according to the type of touch they detect. Meissner's sensors are near the surface and respond to very light pressure. Pacinian sensors detect heavier pressure and are lower down.

MICRO-SENSORS

Skin protects the body from knocks, harmful rays and germs, keeps in body fluids, and stops the body getting too hot or cold. But skin is also the main touch organ of the body. An area of skin the size of a fingernail has up to one million microscopic touch sensors. These are the specially shaped ends of nerve fibres, sited just under the surface. There are at least seven main kinds of sensors. The largest are the size of a pinhead, but most are thousands of times smaller. Each detects different features of touch. Some respond to very light contact,

others to heavier pressure, or heat, cold or vibrations. Yet other kinds of sensors respond to all of these. The sensors send complicated patterns of nerve signals to the brain. A strip-shaped area on either side of the brain's surface, the touch centre or somato-sensory cortex, works out the type of object or substance which is being touched.

Try this!

Very carefully, move a tiny hair on your arm, without contacting the skin there. Can you feel anything? The hair itself is dead and has no sense of touch. But wrapped around its base, in the skin, are sensitive nerve endings. They detect that hair's movement. When a strong wind blows on the skin, we feel it because it rocks the tiny hairs there.

A vital warning

Pain is perhaps the most unwelcome of the body's senses – yet it is vital. It warns that a body part is damaged or injured. Pain tells us to be careful and to take action, to limit the damage and allow the part to heal itself. If we ignore the pain of a wound in the skin, the wound may worsen and, left open, become infected with germs. If we take no note of the pain in a damaged joint, we may continue to use the joint, rather than resting it, and increase the harm.

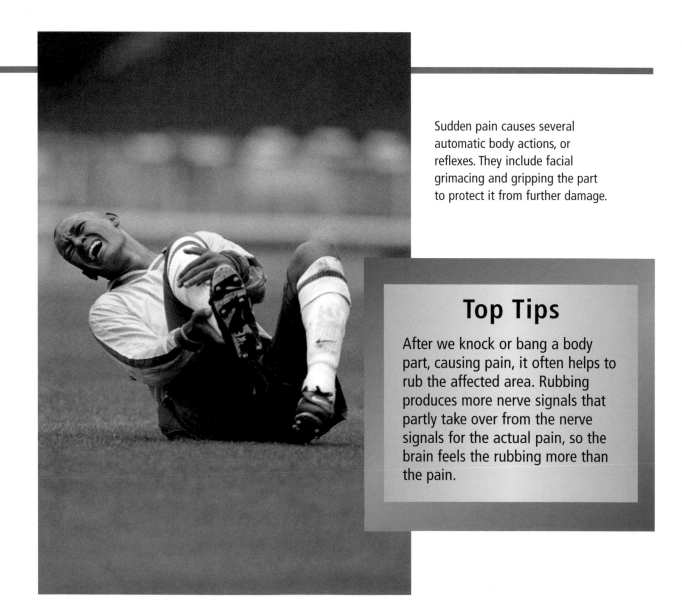

Sudden pain causes several automatic body actions, or reflexes. They include facial grimacing and gripping the part to protect it from further damage.

Top Tips

After we knock or bang a body part, causing pain, it often helps to rub the affected area. Rubbing produces more nerve signals that partly take over from the nerve signals for the actual pain, so the brain feels the rubbing more than the pain.

PAIN ALL OVER

Pain is part of the sense of touch, based in the skin. But it can also occur in almost any body part – in joints, muscles, blood vessels, the stomach, nerves, even deep inside bones. All of these parts have microscopic nerve fibre endings specialized to detect damage around them. They are shaped like tiny branching trees, and are called free nerve endings. Oddly, the only part of the body that lacks these pain sensors is the brain. So the brain detects pain in other body parts, but it cannot feel any damage or harm to itself.

── **weblinks** ──
To find out more about touch and pain sensors, go to www.waylinks.co.uk/series/ourbodies/senses

The tree-like branches of a free nerve ending pass through the skin, waiting to respond to any damage.

TYPES OF PAIN

No one can experience the pain felt by another person. But we can describe our pain to others, with words such as sharp, shooting, burning, crushing, cramping, dull, aching and throbbing. We can also say if a pain comes and goes or is there all the time, and whether it stops us doing anything. It is important to describe all of these aspects of pain clearly to a doctor or other medical worker, since the description can give clues to the cause and extent of the underlying problem.

MICRO-BODY

Free nerve endings are the tiny, branching ends of nerve fibres. They are found in most body parts and detect not only pain but also heat, cold and movements.

BALANCE

A continuous process
Balance is sometimes called the 'sixth sense', in addition to the main five senses. But it is really a body process that goes on all the time, using information from various sense organs.

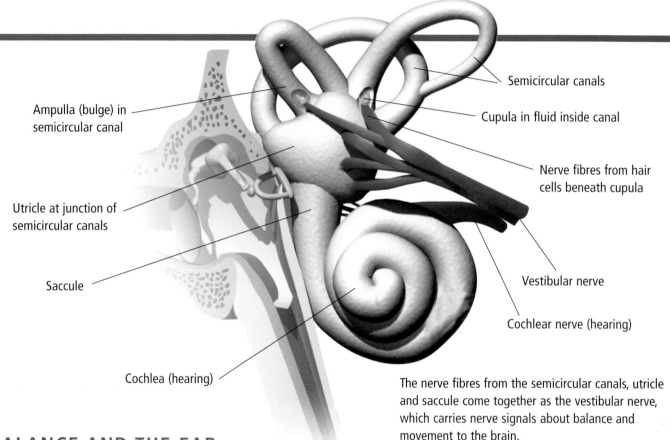

Ampulla (bulge) in semicircular canal

Utricle at junction of semicircular canals

Saccule

Cochlea (hearing)

Semicircular canals

Cupula in fluid inside canal

Nerve fibres from hair cells beneath cupula

Vestibular nerve

Cochlear nerve (hearing)

The nerve fibres from the semicircular canals, utricle and saccule come together as the vestibular nerve, which carries nerve signals about balance and movement to the brain.

BALANCE AND THE EAR

Inside the ear, joined to the cochlea are bulging parts called the utricle and saccule, and three C-shaped tubes, the semicircular canals. Like the cochlea, these are filled with fluid. The utricle and saccule contain jelly-like lumps of tiny, heavy crystals called otoconia. Microscopic hair cells, like those in the cochlea, have tiny hairs that stick into these lumps. The force of gravity pulls the lumps down. As the head changes position, the angle of pull alters, moving the micro-hairs so that their cells send nerve signals to the brain.

Each semicircular canal also has a bulge near one end, containing another patch of hair cells. Their micro-hairs stick into another jelly-like lump, the cupula. As the head twists and turns, the fluid in each canal swishes to and fro. This pushes the cupula, which pulls on the hair cells and so makes nerve signals. The three canals are at right angles to each other. So any head movement – up-down, side-side, front-back – affects one or more of the canals.

OTHER ASPECTS OF BALANCE

Sight and touch help balance. The eyes see horizontal surfaces like floors and water surfaces, and vertical ones like walls and tree-trunks. As the head tilts, these change angles, and the brain notes this. Also as the body leans, pressure on the feet and other body parts alters, and again the brain receives information about this (see next page). From all these sensory inputs, the brain works out the position and movement of the body, and instructs muscles to keep it poised and 'well-balanced'.

Try this!

Stand up straight and close your eyes. Gradually you may feel your body start to lean or sway. Your brain has lost one set of sensory inputs which help with balance – from your eyes. So staying upright becomes slightly more difficult, and soon you want to open your eyes again.

PROBLEMS WITH BALANCE

When you cannot control your balance, for instance on a theme park ride, the messages going to your brain can make you feel dizzy and sick. Inner ear infections can also affect the balance organs there and can cause the same sorts of symptoms.

Jet pilots train to become used to sudden changes in direction and position, so their balance is less affected.

WHERE AM I?

A sense of position

Do you know, without looking at your hand, what position it is in? Is your wrist straight, and are your fingers together or spread apart? Somehow you 'know' the position of a body part, even though you cannot see it. This positional sense is called proprioception or the kinaesthetic sense. It tells the brain about the position or posture of each part. This sense comes from millions of microscopic sensors throughout the body, linked to the brain by nerves.

The brain can detect the positions and tiny movements of the fingers, without seeing, using the proprioceptive sense – renowned musician Stevie Wonder has no vision.

Top Tips

When body parts have stayed in the same position for some time, it is good to stretch and bend them. This prevents blood vessels and nerves becoming kinked, relieves tension in muscles and joints, and helps the proprioceptive sensors to 'update' the brain about the body's posture.

SPRAYS AND SPINDLES

Proprioceptive sensors are mostly less than one-tenth of one millimetre in size, and they have various names and shapes. They include 'spray' nerve endings shaped like little trees, 'corpuscle' nerve endings which are rounded with layers (like tiny onions), and 'spindle' nerve endings which are long and tapering. These sensors are especially common in muscles and joints. They constantly detect the amount of pull or stretch, which alters as the body moves, and send their nerve signals to the brain.

SQUASH AND STRETCH

The information from this inner proprioceptive sense is especially important in providing information for balance. For example, as you stand up and lean forwards, the pressure on the front of your feet increases, and you feel this in the skin on the foot. But the sensors in the muscles and joints also respond by feeling the pressure, all the way up the front of your feet, legs and main body. Meanwhile, the muscles around the back of the legs and main body are stretched slightly. Proprioceptive sensors detect all this and inform the brain.

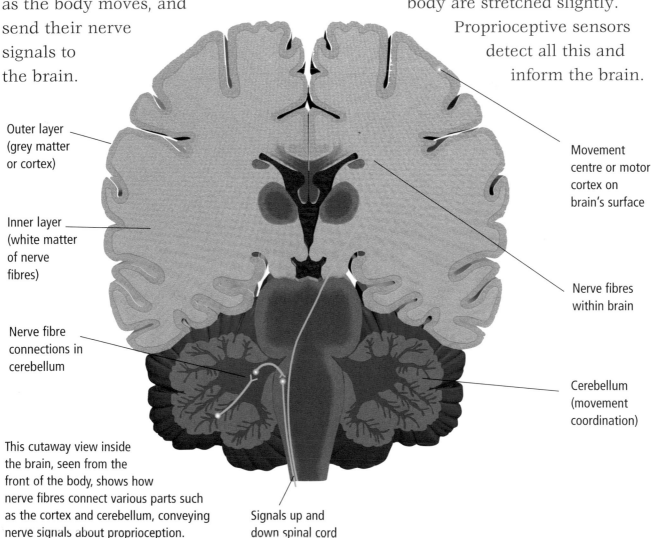

Outer layer (grey matter or cortex)

Inner layer (white matter of nerve fibres)

Nerve fibre connections in cerebellum

Movement centre or motor cortex on brain's surface

Nerve fibres within brain

Cerebellum (movement coordination)

This cutaway view inside the brain, seen from the front of the body, shows how nerve fibres connect various parts such as the cortex and cerebellum, conveying nerve signals about proprioception.

Signals up and down spinal cord

A FIVE-SENSES EXPERIENCE

MMMM ... DELICIOUS!

Next time you start a tasty meal, pause for a moment. Your enjoyment of food comes from your senses – and they all work alongside each other during the eating experience. The first hint of food might be the odours of cooking, which float from the oven or hob, through the air to your nose – even if you are some distance away. As explained earlier, smells can cause powerful reactions. The odour of food often makes the body prepare to eat, by causing the release of saliva (spit) into the mouth, ready for chewing. This is why we say a meal 'smells mouth-watering'. You can also hear the sounds of cooking, such as the crackle and spit of the grill. Sounds and smells are useful because they work 'around corners' and can carry from room to room, from places which the eyes cannot see.

MORE AND MORE SENSES

Experienced cooks often say that we 'eat with our eyes'. If a meal looks well presented and appetizing, we are more likely to enjoy it. Sight is very important for checking the meal too.

Are you feeling hungry? Even the sight of food in a photograph can tempt the appetite and make us ready to eat.

For example, if the peas on a plate were blue or the baked beans were green, we would be suspicious. Then as we start to eat, the food is chewed and mixed with saliva, which releases more odorant and flavorant substances, so tastes and smells can combine for further enjoyment.

Touch is involved, too. There are micro-sensors, similar to those in the skin, on the lips, tongue and gums, and in the lining of the cheeks and other mouth parts. These enable us to feel whether the food is hot or cold, hard or squishy, and other features of its texture or consistency. A meal is a full five-senses experience. It shows how the body's senses are vital for our pleasure and enjoyment, as well as for finding out information and what is happening around us – and for our basic survival.

ANIMAL VERSUS HUMAN

The human body has deep-seated reactions and instincts to avoid certain foods, especially old, rotting meat. But wild creatures such as the leopard are adapted to cope with such meals. This big cat may leave part of its prey, such as a gazelle, in a tree for a week or two, in the hot sun – and then come back to eat the decaying, smelly meat.

The odour of old raw meat would make us wrinkle our noses and turn away. Generally, people prefer sweeter foods, especially when we are young.

GLOSSARY

capillary The smallest type of blood vessel, much thinner than a human hair, with walls only one cell thick.

cell A single unit or 'building block' of life – the human body is made of billions of cells of many different kinds.

cilia Microscopic hair-like parts that can waft or wave to and fro, such as those lining the nasal chambers inside the nose.

cochlea A small, snail-shaped part deep inside the ear, which changes the vibrations of sounds into nerve signals.

cone Short, tapering cell in the retina of the eye, specialized to make nerve signals when various colours of light fall on it.

convergence In eyesight, when the eyes turn or swivel inwards slightly so they both look directly at a nearby object.

cortex The outermost wrinkled layer of the brain, where most conscious thoughts and sensations happen.

ear canal The tube or tunnel leading from the outer ear on the side of the head, inwards to the eardrum.

epithelium A layer covering the surface of a body part or forming its inner lining.

flavorants Tiny particles of substances or chemicals, too small to see, in foods and drinks, which stimulate the taste buds on the tongue and give us the sensation of taste.

fovea Small area in the middle of the retina of the eye, which has most cone cells for sharpest, clearest vision.

ganglion A lump-like part of a nerve which contains a group or gathering of the cell bodies from nerve cells.

gustatory To do with the sense of taste.

hallucinations When a person experiences sights, sounds, smells, tastes or touches, and these are not produced in the usual way from outside the body, but from within, usually in the brain or mind.

humour A general name for a liquid or fluid in the body, such as vitreous humour, the clear, jelly-like fluid inside the eyeball.

impulse A tiny surge or pulse of electricity that passes along a nerve, also called a nerve signal or nerve message.

iris A coloured ring shape of muscle at the front of the eye, with a hole in the middle called the pupil.

mucus General name for various thick, slimy, gooey fluids made by the body, especially to coat and protect the surfaces of its inner parts.

nerves Long, thin, string-like parts inside the body, which carry information in the form of nerve impulses or signals.

odorants Tiny particles of substances or chemicals, too small to see, which float in the air and stimulate the olfactory cells in the nose, to give us the sensation of smell.

olfactory To do with the sense of smell.

optic To do with the sense of sight (vision).

ossicles The three tiny bones deep in each ear, which pass vibrations from the eardrum to the cochlea.

papillae Small lump- or pimple-like parts on the surface of a body part such as the tongue.

proprioception A sensory process within the body that tells us the position, angle and posture of body parts like the fingers, hands, arms, back and legs.

pupil A hole in the iris at the front of the eye, which lets light into the eyeball.

retina The very thin, bowl-shaped layer inside the rear of the eyeball, which detects patterns of light rays and makes nerve signals.

rod Long, thin cell in the retina of the eye, specialized to make nerve signals when light falls on it.

saccule A bag-shaped part filled with fluid deep in the ear, which senses the movements of the head and makes nerve signals.

saliva The watery liquid made by six salivary glands inside the face, which moistens the mouth and pours onto food to help chewing and swallowing.

sclera The tough outer covering of the eyeball.

semicircular canals Three C-shaped tubes filled with fluid deep in the ear, which sense the movements of the head and make nerve signals.

somato-sensory cortex Parts on the cortex (outer surface) of the brain which receive and analyze nerve signals about touch and feeling from the skin.

utricle A box-shaped part filled with fluid deep in the ear, which senses the movements of the head and makes nerve signals.

FURTHER INFORMATION

BOOKS

Smell, Hearing, Touch, Taste, Sight (five title series), Patricia J Murphy (True Book: Health and the Human Body, 2003)

The Ear: Learning How We Hear, Josepha Sherman (Rosen Publishing Group, 2002)

The Eye: Learning How We See, Jennifer Viegas (Rosen Publishing Group, 2002)

The Musculoskeletal System and the Skin, Susan Dudley Gold (Enslow Publishers Inc, 2003)

Why Do I Get Sunburn: And Other Questions About Skin, Angela Royston (Heinemann Library, 2003)

ORGANIZATIONS

RNIB – Royal National Institute of the Blind
The leading charity offering information, support and advice to over two million blind and partially sighted people in the UK.

RNIB Customer Services, PO Box 173, Peterborough PE2 6WS
Tel: 020 7388 1266
RNIB Helpline: 0845 766 99 99 Monday to Friday 9 am to 5 pm

RNID – Royal National Institute for the Deaf
The largest organization representing the 8.7 million deaf and hard of hearing people in the UK.

19–23 Featherstone Street, London EC1Y 8SL
Tel: 020 7296 8000
RNID Information Line: 0808 808 0123 (freephone)

National Deaf Children's Society
NDCS is a UK organization of parents, families and carers which exists to support parents in enabling children with hearing loss to maximize their skills and abilities.

15 Dufferin Street, London, EC1Y 8UR
Tel: 020 7490 8656

National Blind Children's Society
A UK charity providing information, advice, support and services to blind and partially sighted children.

Bradbury House, Market Street, Highbridge, Somerset TA9 3BW
Tel: 01278 764 764

INDEX